ELT **Development Series**

SERIES EDITOR Thomas S. C. Farrell

Sociolinguistics and Language Teaching

Thomas S. C. Farrell

www.tesol.org/bookstore

TESOL International Association
1925 Ballenger Avenue
Alexandria, Virginia, 22314 USA
www.tesol.org

Director of Publishing and Product Development: Myrna Jacobs
Copy Editor: Sarah Duffy
Cover: Citrine Sky Design
Interior Design & Layout: Capitol Communications, LLC
Printing: Gasch Printing, LLC

ISBN 978-1-942799-88-7
Library of Congress Control Number 2017950155

Table of Contents

Series Editor's Preface

The English Language Teacher Development (ELTD) Series consists of a set of short resource books for ESL/EFL teachers that are written in a jargon free and accessible manner for all types of teachers of English (native, non-native, experienced and novice teachers). The ELTD series is designed to offer teachers a theory-to-practice approach to second language teaching and each book offers a wide variety range of practical teaching approaches and methods of the topic at hand. Each book also offers time for reflections for each teacher to interact with the materials presented in the book. The books can be used in pre-service settings or in in-service courses and can also be used by individual looking for ways to refresh their practice.

Thomas Farrell's book *Sociolinguistics and Language Teaching* explores various methods and approaches of how sociolinguistics can inform language teaching. Farrell shows how sociolinguistics, a sub-discipline of linguistics (and not developed originally for TESOL), is very relevant to TESOL as we recognized that language learning does not take place in a social vacuum. Sociolinguistic topics as they relate to language teaching covered include: multilingualism, which and whose English? gender and language and identity and language planning. *Sociolinguistics and Language Teaching* is another valuable addition to the literature in our profession and to the ELTD series.

I am very grateful to the authors who contributed to the ELTD Series for sharing their knowledge and expertize with other TESOL professionals. It is truly an honor for me to work with each of these authors as they selflessly gave up their valuable time for the advancement of TESOL.

Thomas S. C. Farrell

CHAPTER 1

Sociolinguistics and Language Teaching

People use language to interact and communicate with each other, and there are many different languages in the world with many different speakers of each language. Most people speak at least one dominant language, but many are bilingual or trilingual. When people want to travel or study in a different country whose speakers use a language different than their first language, they must consider learning that country's language as a second or foreign language. Over the years many organizations (e.g., TESOL, IATEFL) have formalized in some way how teachers and students can engage in teaching and learning second and foreign languages.

Of course, many different approaches and methods of teaching and learning these foreign languages, including English, have been proposed over the years, sometimes with great controversy. As the knowledge-base of teaching English to speakers of other languages (TESOL) has greatly expanded in the past two decades, language educators (but not publishers) have begun to take notice that it is no longer useful or acceptable to just teach language in isolation as a rule-governed activity without any focus on the sociocultural components that can affect second language learners (Folse & Vitanova, 2006). As Folse and Vitanova (2006) have correctly pointed out, when teaching English "we need to consider much more than grammar rules, vocabulary lists, reading comprehension quizzes, or essays" (p. 49).

They maintain that TESOL programs should add sociolinguistics components (e.g., dialects and registers, speech acts, world Englishes, gender) to the traditional English language teaching courses to aid instructors who are in either the preservice or in-service phases of their careers.

It is my belief that knowledge of sociolinguistics can enlighten and inform parents, students, teachers, administrators, politicians, and national leaders. This knowledge can hopefully lead all to adopt a more tolerant rather than exclusionary view to differences in attitudes about how people speak their second language given that most will have been socialized in many ways that are different than what is expected in the English-speaking world. This book outlines what sociolinguistics is, its relevance to TESOL, and why it is important to be included in TESOL teacher education and development programs.

REFLECTIVE QUESTIONS

- What is sociolinguistics?

- How is it relevant to TESOL?

What Is Sociolinguistics?

Sociolinguistics, a subdiscipline of linguistics, is basically the study of the relationship between language and society (Holmes, 2008). It is concerned about how language is used by real people in real social settings and how this can be described rather than judged. It is important to point out, however, that sociolinguistics was not originally developed with TESOL or teaching any other second language in mind, and some scholars within this subdiscipline want to maintain it as a separate entity from language teaching. Nevertheless, most agree that research results for sociolinguistics help address social problems such as miscommunication, bias, oppression, conflicts, and professional training as well as inform language teaching. It is this final point that we are concerned with in this book: how sociolinguistics can inform language teaching. As Bayyurt (2013) has noted, sociolinguistics "attempts to explain how language differs from one context to another across geographical borders and how people in one context communicate with people in other contexts (e.g., nonnative-nonnative speakers; nonnative-native speakers)" (p. 70), which is very relevant to TESOL.

The Role of TESOL Teachers

A pertinent question at this stage is: How is the study of sociolinguistics relevant to the TESOL profession? Although I mentioned above that socio-linguistics did not develop with language teaching in mind, the research it produces is relevant to the field of TESOL. In a very early (and trend-setting) article, Shuy (1969) attempted to establish the relevance of sociolinguistics in TESOL by underscoring the importance of researchers and educators alike in recognizing the "systematicity," linguistic features, and strategies for analyzing language, in particular the minority language of socioeconomi-cally disadvantaged children. Two of Shuy's main goals were to establish the legitimacy of nonstandard forms of language and to change the mindset of educators who view the speech of the minority language child, for example, as "deviant from the standard norm" (p. 14). Shuy continued that the "inability of teachers to describe nonstandard language with any degree of diagnostic usefulness has suggested that we try to discover the vocabulary of socially meaningful terms with which people can evaluate speech" (p. 16). However, in the intervening years we may wonder how research in sociolin-guistics has actually impacted the field of TESOL. I would suggest that not until relatively recently was it recognized that language learning does not take place in a social vacuum and that sociolinguistics is in fact very relevant to TESOL (Bayyurt, 2013; Folse & Vitanova, 2006).

REFLECTIVE QUESTIONS

- Why do you think Shuy (1969), even at that time, maintained that it would be difficult to change trained teachers' attitudes toward language learning and teaching?

- How and why are these attitudes ingrained?

Folse and Vitanova (2006) point out that it is important for TESOL teachers to be knowledgeable about sociolinguistics and especially issues such as dialects and registers, world Englishes, and gender and language, to name but a few. Folse and Vitanova maintain that it is important for language teachers to be aware of social dialects because such awareness can influence their approach to language teaching, not only as a way to eliminate any personal biases toward a certain variety, but also so that they can help their students develop awareness of a multitude of varieties and dialects of English. As Folse and Vitanova state: "English language learners, particularly those who have studied in an EFL setting, may be confused by the diversity they encounter in language use by native speakers of English" (p. 51). Indeed, they go on to suggest that language teachers should "examine their own views about 'correctness' and . . . disperse some common stereotypes about language varieties that are different from Standard English" (p. 51). Awareness also applies in relation to registers, as learners need to know about appropriate degrees of formality that are tied to the social context of speech (Folse & Vitanova, 2006).

Folse and Vitanova (2006) also note the importance of awareness of the idea of "correctness" and the concept of world Englishes and different varieties of English that serve different purposes in a specific region or community of speakers: "While numerous differences exist between these different Englishes, the important teaching point is that no variety of English is "correct" (p. 53). One other important area of sociolinguistics that they suggest requires attention by TESOL is that of gender in language teaching, specifically how it relates to English grammar and how learners should avoid sexist language: "Sociolinguistic studies are concerned not only with the gender identity of the language learners but also linguistic features within the English language, especially sexist language and specific suggestions for avoiding it" (p. 54).

So Folse and Vitanova (2006) provide a useful summary of just some of the important sociocultural aspects that should be brought to the attention of the TESOL profession. However, although they have made a strong case for why sociolinguistic research has relevance for TESOL, as Bayyurt (2013) has observed, for the most part, "sociolinguistics has been an ignored or overlooked area of study" (p. 71).

REFLECTIVE QUESTIONS

- Do you think that sociolinguistic research has been ignored in TESOL?

- If yes, what kind of research?

Conclusion

This book will review various aspects of sociolinguistic research that are essential for language teachers to be aware of so that they can benefit in their language teaching and their students can benefit in their language learning. More specifically, this book will cover the following sociolinguistic topics as they relate to language teaching: multilingualism, which English? whose English?, gender and language and identity, and language planning.

CHAPTER 2

Multilingualism

I got a phone call one day from the mother of a young elementary student in Canada who worried about the use of different languages at home and in school. This was a new immigrant family from Poland, and the young girl's mother had just returned from a meeting with the child's second grader's ESL teacher, who told the mother that she and her husband should speak only English at home with the child if she is to assimilate into the class and the country. In addition, the teacher said that speaking one language at home and a different language in class was harmful for the child's overall linguistic and psychological development because the child would be confused about both languages as well as both cultures. The mother asked me for advice because she got my phone number from one of my previous students. I will tell you what my response was after you answer the following reflective questions. After that, the chapter introduces the concept of multilingualism and code-switching by both students and teachers of ESL.

REFLECTIVE QUESTIONS

- What would you have done if you received such a phone call? Should the parents speak only English at home?

- Do you think multilingualism can cause some confusion for students who are trying to acquire English as an additional language?

- Do you think TESOL teachers have a role to play in fostering multilingual behavior in the classroom? If yes, what actions do you think they should take? If no, why not?

Now that you have reflected on the issue of the parents who immigrated to Canada and sought my guidance about raising their child speaking two (or more) languages in their home from an early age, I will relate what I advised. Basically, I told the mother that from my knowledge of research in linguistics, speaking the native language at home would not harm the child in her development (although it may slow it slightly); rather, this approach would provide the child with better cognitive functions in the long run, especially metacognitive abilities and the ability to compare different languages and perhaps employ different learning strategies. However, I also pointed out that parents develop an emotional bond with their children from birth, and the language they use from the beginning for the most part remains their emotional language and their connection. Thus, I wanted to reassure the parents that they should continue to speak their home language as this is their emotional connection when communicating. I agree with De Angelis (2011) that "discouraging immigrant families from using a home language will ultimately lead to a double loss: the loss of the home language and the loss of the potential cognitive benefits that may arise out of being a speaker of two or more languages" (p. 217).

I realize also that this is not all straightforward for families wondering what to do in this situation. They need assurance and guidance about raising their child in a multilingual setting. Ultimately, I believe TESOL teachers have a role to play here in fostering and encouraging multilingual behavior in the language classroom, and their actions can have a positive influence on their students' learning of English. In this chapter I will briefly outline what multilingualism is and how TESOL teachers can play an important (pedagogical) role in the classroom as well as outside the classroom when giving advice and encouragement to families about how and when to use the home language in their daily lives.

The Role of TESOL Teachers

Multilingual people speak more than one language and as a result are different from monolingual people, who only speak one language. First, they notice that the languages they speak are different in many ways (metalinguistic ability) and that they can draw on one of their languages when learning another language; monolingual people cannot. As De Angelis (2011) points out that "having knowledge of more than one language seems to lead to a heightened awareness of language and to the development of metalinguistic abilities which are put to use during the learning process" (p. 218). However, to say that multilingual people learn languages better as a result of their learning strategies may be a bit of a stretch, and the extent of being multilingual and better at language learning is still under debate (Haukås, 2016).

That said, in language classes in particular, language teachers can play an important role in promoting and supporting multilingualism among students (De Angelis, 2011). De Angelis (2011) suggests that teachers can impact policy by choosing to integrate minority languages into their teaching, thus "turning students' multilingualism into a useful resource for the entire classroom," or they "can choose to ignore minority languages closing a source of linguistic knowledge for their students" (p. 217). Even if we think we agree that language teachers have an important role to play in English language learners' multilingualism, Haukås (2016) has pointed out that surprisingly little research is available that focuses on teachers' knowledge and beliefs about multilingualism and appropriate multilingual pedagogical approaches they can use.

Previous research on fostering multilingualism in a classroom indicated that, in general, teachers have positive attitude toward multilingualism and its benefits. However, most of the teachers acknowledged that they do not encourage the use of other languages in their classrooms due to their fears that this might delay the learning of the majority of students. Haukås (2016) set out to get information about language teachers in four schools in Norway with third language (L3) language ability concerning their beliefs about whether multilingualism is as an asset for language learning. Haukås also wanted to know the extent to which language teachers draw on their learners' previous linguistic knowledge and collaborate with other language teachers to enhance learners' multilingualism.

REFLECTIVE QUESTIONS

- Do you agree or disagree with this teacher's statement: "It's not my job to help students maintain their heritage language."

- To what extent do you draw on your learners' previous linguistic knowledge?

- Do you make reference to the home language or culture of the immigrant students in your class?

- To what extent do you collaborate with other language teachers to enhance learners' multilingualism?

You can now compare your answers with what Haukås (2016) found. During the focus group discussions, the teachers were asked to reflect on the following statement: "The more languages you know, the easier it is to learn new languages." All of the teachers regarded this statement as especially true when thinking about their own history of language learning. In addition, when the teachers were asked to describe what knowledge learners had would be ideally transferred from their previous language learning, most of the teachers stated that more knowledge of grammar and terminology would be useful. Indeed, the teachers said that they regarded multilingualism not only as positive for learners but also as a great tool to help learners find linguistic links between the L3 and previously learned languages (primarily first language [L1] Norwegian and second language [L2] English). However, for most of the teachers the use of the multilingual pedagogical approach stops there because they tend not to reflect on previous language learning experiences with their students. Furthermore, they stated that there is no collaboration between language teachers to increase the strength of learners' multilingualism.

In another interesting study in a K–12 context in California, Lee and Oxelson (2006) investigated 69 public school teachers' attitudes toward their students' heritage language maintenance and their engagement in classroom practices that may or may not affirm the value of maintaining

Sociolinguistics and Language Teaching

and developing such heritage languages among students. The researchers discovered that most teachers reported it was not their job, citing three reasons: "(1) They saw it as a personal or family activity; (2) They did not have time in class to address the issues; and (3) They did not know how to support heritage language maintenance" (p. 465). However, Lee and Oxelson maintain that it is vital for the overall development of the child that teachers consider the important of their students' heritage language:

> We argue that teachers' recognition of the importance of heritage languages in the lives of their linguistic minority students is critical to the development and empowerment of the whole child and that heritage language maintenance needs to become more visible in the agendas of educators. (p. 468)

The use of students' L1 in the English language classroom is a much-debated topic, and Haukås's (2016) discovered that "the majority of teachers were hesitant to bring other languages into the classroom unless they were familiar with them" (p. 3). In fact, what we have in the field of TESOL is something of a paradox: On the one hand many teachers are generally reluctant to allow students to use their L1, or code-switch, while on the other hand many also encourage the preservation of students' home languages.

Code-switching can be generally defined as "the alternation and mixing of languages within a conversational utterance" (Dewaele & Wei, 2014, p. 235). People have both positive and negative attitudes toward its use in everyday conversation. From a negative perspective, for example, Dewaele and Wei (2014) report studies using pejorative terms for code-switching such as "verbal salad" (Nigeria), "still colonized" (Morocco), and "very irritating" (Hong Kong) as well as it being dismissed by monolinguals as "gibberish." They also note some seemingly neutral-sounding terms such as "Tex-Mex," "Franglais," "Japlish," "Singlish," and "Chinglish," to name but a few; however, these also have negative connotations associated with "inferior" English. These terms seem to reflect the ideologies of monolinguals who have no understanding of another language and feel threatened when they do not understand two or more people speaking and code-switching into a common language with each other. This could also be the result of some people believing in a pure form of their language and not wanting any other language thrown into a conversation, which reflects linguistic purism (Dewaele & Wei, 2014), or one language only (OLON) and one language at a time (OLAT). Some people also believe that languages are best kept separate so they can be well formed without any interference and that code-switching can reflect laziness or poor proficiency in the language being learned.

REFLECTIVE QUESTIONS

- If you speak more than one language, do you code-switch? If yes, why?

- When do you code-switch?

- Do you think code-switching reflects linguistic laziness and/or poor proficiency?

- Why do you think some monolingual and/or bilingual people have a negative attitude toward code-switching?

In a more positive light, code-switching promotes multilingualism, and its use in the classroom suggests that that all languages are equal and there is no one language that is better than the other (House, 2003). As House (2003) notes: "If one makes the distinction between languages for communication, such as English today, and language for identification—mother tongues, regional, local, intimate varieties of language—ELF [English as a lingua franca] need not be a threat" (p. 562). For example, House notes the benefits of students using their L1 in the classroom, such as allowing them to make a connection between the two languages and transferring skills from their L1 to their L2. Code-switching can also indicate a sign of linguistic creativity, as the student speaker makes an adjustment to his or her language choice depending on the communicative demand in the L2 at that time.

There are also benefits for teachers, such as when code-switching enables them to save time in explaining directions, highlight important information, and manage student behavior in the classroom when all speakers have the same L1 background (Liu, Ahn, Baek, & Han, 2004). However, there are some who point out the need to establish some frameworks for allowing both students and teachers to code-switch in the language classroom. Macaro (2001), for example, has pointed out that it is necessary to establish parameters of L2/L1 use and provide teachers, especially less experienced teachers, with "a framework that identifies when reference to the L1 can be a valuable tool and when it is simply used as an easy option" (p. 545). Thus it is imperative that each teacher determines that when students code-switch it is for linguistic development rather than a comfortable way out of using the target language.

Lee (2012) has developed an interesting preliminary model of effectiveness of code-switching for teachers that he says can act as "a pedagogical compass with which teachers can make judicious and an effective use of CS [code-switching]" (p. 153). Lee explains each of the four aspects of the model as follows:

- *Learners' ages/proficiency levels:* Learners of different ages and different proficiency levels in the L2 will be impacted differently by a teacher's use of code-switching in the classroom. Most likely, older learners will have more strategies to use when in target-language–only classrooms, while younger learners may require more use of a teacher's code-switching because they do not have such learning strategies when trying to comprehend the target language.

- *Learners' attitudes toward code-switching and target-language–only instruction:* Students' learning outcomes can be mediated by their attitudes toward teachers' language in instruction and connections between the effectiveness of teacher code-switching.

- *Target language areas and required information categories:* Previous research on teachers' use of code-switching has been narrowly focused on grammar and vocabulary, so future second language acquisition research on the use of code-switching should be expanded to investigate the effect of code-switching/target-language–only instruction on learners' acquisition of abstract and concrete words.

- *Practical considerations:* Given the time limit of each lesson and the number of students in each class with a vast array of linguistic differences, teachers may vary in their effective use of code-switching when teaching the target language. Such practical considerations are not likely to be independent of the effectiveness of teacher code-switching.

Lee (2012) maintains that when adapting this model, teachers and researchers should also consider the effects of teacher code-switching in classrooms where the target language, not the learners' first language, is the primary language of instruction and where the main lesson activities are communicative in nature and meaning focused rather than form focused.

REFLECTIVE QUESTIONS

- Do you code-switch when teaching? If yes, when and why? If no, why not?

- Some language schools and teachers have a policy of banning L1 use or fining students who do not always speak English in class. What is your view of this?

- Lee (2012) outlines what he calls an "all-too-typical scenario" in modern target language classrooms:

  Consider the example of a female English teacher who is forced to adhere to an administrative policy of "English-exclusivity" in her EFL classroom with primary level students who share the same first language with her. Her students frequently get bogged down by not being able to understand the messages which their teacher delivers via English-only instruction, and pretend they understand when in fact they do not. The teacher sometimes wonders why she cannot serve as a target model of an individual who has successfully learned and easily uses two languages— a competent bilingual, instead of effectively disguising herself as a monolingual speaker in her classroom.

  — Is this scenario familiar and typical for you?

  — How would you respond to this policy of "English exclusivity"?

- Lee (2012) has developed a preliminary model of effective teacher code-switching (see above). Comment on its usefulness for your context.

Conclusion

Some people (including teachers) still believe that one language may interfere with the learning of another, despite the research that shows that bi/multilingualism facilitates the acquisition of additional languages and improves cognitive functioning (De Angelis, 2011). Multilingualism is an asset in any language program, and TESOL teachers have an important role to play when facilitating their students' linguistic awareness across the languages each student knows. TESOL teachers can create teaching materials that encourage their students to draw on their knowledge of other languages when learning English. Teachers can also help students develop a positive attitude toward multilingualism by allowing them to use their L1 in the classroom if they need to use it and treat this usage as linguistic creativity rather than penalizing students. However, each teacher must decide when to allow students to use their L1 as a valuable tool rather than an easy way out.

CHAPTER 3

Which English?
Whose English?

English is the most widely spoken language around the world if we consider those who speak it as a first, second, third, and other language. Of course, there are quite a few varieties of English available for speakers to choose from, but many learners of English as an additional language tend to try to follow a so-called standard variety. Sometimes, though, it is not up to the learners to choose which variety as this decision has already been made for them by policy-makers, textbook publishers and curricula specialists, language education programs, and materials writers. The usual dichotomy of language models to follow is the so-called native-speaker models from countries that use English as their first language (e.g., United States, United Kingdom, Australia, New Zealand) as opposed to the nonnative-speaker models from countries that use English as an additional language (e.g., Singapore, Malaysia). It all depends on who will decide on what variety and who will act as the gatekeepers when making such a decision: government institutions, examination boards, universities, publishers, teachers, learners, and so on. In this chapter I focus mostly on the role of the teacher: perceptions, attitudes, and policies in terms of the variety of English promoted in the TESOL classroom. First, I discuss the different varieties of English used as a first language and then as an additional language. This is followed by a discussion of the role of the teacher in terms of what variety of English to teach.

Varieties of English

Most languages, including English, have varieties that can be called dialects. Dialects can be noticed in English in terms of pronunciation, vocabulary usage, and grammar differences. We can all notice these in the different type or dialect of English used in the United States and the United Kingdom, or so-called American English and British English—although dialect usually refers to differences of grammar and vocabulary, generally accent denotes differences in pronunciation. However, there are also different varieties of English used within these contexts, such as southern English as opposed to English used in New York City, or English in northern England and English used in London. Of course, within these contexts we have also heard the terms *standard* and *nonstandard* use of English, which assumes that we all have the same interpretation of what standard and nonstandard mean.

When primary school teachers tell students to use standard English, this suggests that we all share a similar understanding of exactly what this means, yet as Farrell and Martin (2009) point out, "it is not easy to define" (p. 2). Indeed, a Canadian's definition of what standard is may vary dramatically from that of an Irish person, and there are differences between standard American English and standard British English. Standard English obviously carries a certain amount of prestige and is recognized as being socially more acceptable that the nonstandard variety. This indicates that the elites in each country decide what the most acceptable type or standard of English is because of their social class and material success from using that variety. The economically, politically, and socially powerful in each community decide what type of English is acceptable to them (standard) and what is not correct usage (nonstandard). This standard becomes an educational target in these communities because it is considered the most prestigious. This standard is usually represented as the norm of communication in print, national news broadcasts, and higher education circles. However, because most English speakers speak a variety of regional-influenced versions of the language, so-called standard English, although prestigious and widely understood, is a minority language used within these countries. So standard English is a variety or dialect of English that is considered a desirable norm to use and whose linguistic features in terms of vocabulary and grammar do not reflect the part of the country the "standard" or the user is from.

However, if, as Holmes (2008) suggests, languages are not purely linguistic entities but also serve social and political functions, each country's particular standard also has specific social and political functions; these can sometimes be seen in terms of linguistic identity when we say Canadians speak differently than Americans or New Zealanders speak differently than Australians. So although we talk in terms of a standard English used in many countries, there is no recognized, regionally neutral standard in existence worldwide. We can say that some countries sound similar to each other and thus should be grouped under a so-called American variety or British variety or Australian variety, with associated vocabulary usage and spelling and pronunciation similarities, but with each group portraying a different and distinct linguistic identity.

We have discussed the use of English by first language users or native speakers of English (although I purposely avoided using this term). Let's now turn our attention to speakers of English as an additional language, or those who do not use English as their mother tongue and have thus acquired it after their native language (again I avoid using the term nonnative speaker of English). Additional users of English learn and use English for many different reasons such as study, work, migration, and so on. This is mainly because of the global spread of English as a medium of communication (e.g., Internet), commerce, culture, and education.

How did English make such a global spread in the first place? According to Kachru and Nelson (1996), the global spread of English is the result first of migrations from the present British Isles to Australia, New Zealand, and North America and later of initial colonization of Asia and Africa, where local populations have since continued to expand the role of English in postcolonial times. Thus, there has been tremendous growth in different varieties of English with their own distinctive features that are much different than the standard or even nonstandard varieties discussed earlier. In many of these multilingual countries, such as Malaysia, Singapore, Hong Kong, India, and many African countries, English now serves as the language of wider communication (Holmes, 2008).

The term *World Englishes* is used to identify all these different varieties of English being spoken in three concentric circles as outlined by Kachru and Nelson (1996):

- *The inner circle* comprises countries where English is the first or dominant language: the United States, Britain, Canada, Australia, and New Zealand.

- *The outer circle* comprises countries where English has a long history of institutionalized functions and standing as a language with an important role in education, governance, and literary creativity, such as India, Nigeria, Pakistan, Singapore, South Africa, and Zambia.

- *The expanding circle* comprises countries where English has various roles and is widely studied but for more specific purposes than in the outer circle, including (but certainly not limited to) reading knowledge for scientific and technical purposes; such countries currently include China, Indonesia, Iran, Japan, South Korea, and Nepal.

However, in this concentric circle schematization, the different dialects of English not included in the inner circle countries have suffered from a type of stigmatization over the years. This is because some have referred to the English being used in the inner circle countries as standard or native-speaker English, in the outer circle as the English as a second language (ESL) model, and in the expanding circle as the English as a foreign language (EFL) model. This in turn has perpetuated the dichotomy of native-speaker model versus nonnative-speaker model of English, with standard English as the native-speaker model.

Sociolinguistics and Language Teaching

The problem that has arisen is that some people think any use of English beyond the standard variety (i.e., native-speaker model) is considered inferior, but of course insisting on standard English can also devalue other varieties of English in the outer and expanding circle countries. Governments in some of the outer and expanding circle countries then idealize the use of standard English by their citizens, but the simple truth is that standard English as a native-speaker model may be unattainable for many second/foreign language learners. Therefore, it may be unrealistic to use a native-speaker model for language learners.

REFLECTIVE QUESTIONS

- What is your understanding of the type of English used in inner circle, outer circle, and expanding circle countries?

- What is your understanding of the dichotomy of native-speaker versus nonnative-speaker models of English?

- Do you think that native-speaker English should be the attainable desire for speakers in outer and expanding circle countries? Why or why not?

The Role of TESOL Teachers

In an interesting article on the issue of teaching different varieties of English, Young and Walsh (2010) investigated the beliefs of 26 nonnative-English-speaking teachers in Europe, Africa, and West, Southeast, and East Asia, using focus groups and personal interviews, about English variety in learning and teaching. Specifically, they were interested in the teachers' perceptions about the utility of teaching varieties such as English as an international language (EIL) and English as a lingua franca (ELF). Investigating the beliefs of teachers is very important because their beliefs influence their planning and instructional decisions in the classroom and have enormous implications for what their students ultimately learn. Before I get to Young and Walsh's results, I will ask similar questions of you.

The results of Young and Walsh's (2010) interviews indicate that most of the participants had no idea about the varieties that they learned in their countries, although some advanced-level speakers suggested they learned British English and other advanced-level speakers American English. Most (80%) reported that they were teaching an American variety of English and that they did not have a choice about which type to teach. When asked about which type of English they would like to teach, most mentioned a need for standard English. So clearly, the term *standard English* is very much present in the beliefs and minds of nonnative-English-speaking TESOL teachers. Although the majority of participants found the idea of teaching EIL and ELF attractive, Young and Walsh noted that they thought it was impossible to apply in practice and "most participants agreed that this was because most learners did not know what it was" (p. 133). Indeed, all participants expressed a view that they wanted to teach American English because some of the younger people they taught wanted to sound American "to be cool." So regardless of what scholars or others think about what type of English should be taught, there seem to be many other forces at work that may generate other opinions, and not all of them logical as the results of Young and Walsh's study suggest.

With all the competing aspects involved in choosing a variety of English, some balance needs to be achieved between national aims, values, culture, and identity needs as well as an individual's aims, beliefs, and identity needs without choosing one variety over another exclusively. Consequently, Farrell and Martin (2009) have suggested a more balanced approach to English language instruction. They maintain that if only one variety of English is emphasized, regardless of which variety, learners will be disadvantaged. They also recognize that many teachers may not be allowed to decide which variety to teach as it may already be mandated by the government in their context. Thus Farrell and Martin contend that "teachers can inform their practiced about the different varieties of English that exist and consider a balanced approach to teaching English" (p. 4) by considering the following three points:

1. *Consider the teaching context:* With so many varieties to consider, it is best to remember there is no one correct choice for all contexts. Therefore, "the variety of English emphasized should be based on the teaching context, the teachers (including their own teaching abilities and style) as well as the learners' educational and cultural needs" (p. 4).

2. *Value learners' local variety of English:* Regardless of the choice of variety of English being taught, teachers can help their learners understand that this is only one from among many others and that learners' "own English is valuable even though it may differ significantly from what is presented in class" (p. 5).

3. *Prepare learners for intercultural communication:* English language learners will meet many different people from many different contexts and backgrounds who use many different varieties of English. Teachers need to prepare them for these future encounters so that they can understand speakers of varieties of English that differ from their own, thereby focusing on "both *strategic* and *intercultural* competence skills" (p. 5).

REFLECTIVE QUESTIONS

- Should TESOL teachers consider the teaching context when deciding on a variety of English to teach in class?

- Should TESOL teachers value learners' variety of English?

- Should TESOL teachers prepare learners for intercultural communication?

Conclusion

This chapter discussed the idea of different varieties of English and the thorny question of which English variety to teach in the TESOL classroom. The chapter outlined and discussed the notion of standard and nonstandard English as well as the consequences of the global spread of English for communication and other purposes. Some scholars have suggested that English is now used through a schema of countries situated in concentric circles—inner, outer, and expanding—that all produce a different variety of English. What has happened in real life is that English used in the inner circle countries has been characterized as the standard or native-speaker model of English and that many governments, educational institutions, and individual learners have idealized this as the model to learn. However, this model is unattainable for most learners, so the chapter suggests that it is not necessary for teachers to overemphasize standard English; what they should do is to pay more attention to different varieties of English and make efforts to come up with solutions to help students value both their second language and their first language.

CHAPTER 4

Language and Gender

We have come a long way in TESOL from the early 1970s and 1980s, when gender bias was prevalent in many English language textbooks in Western society. This bias against women was focused on anything from exclusion to putting women in a subordinate position and many distortions and even degradation of the position of women in society (including sexist language). By the 1990s gender bias in English language textbooks had become less prevalent, but it still exists today in some countries, some textbooks and teaching materials, and even some classrooms teaching and interaction (e.g., males being called on over females). This chapter outlines and discusses issues related to language and gender (mostly in Western societies) and highlights the role of TESOL teachers when it comes to language and gender in TESOL.

REFLECTIVE QUESTIONS

- What is your understanding of the concept of language and gender?

- What aspects of teaching and learning should be considered when it comes to language and gender in TESOL?

Language and Gender

In terms of language, early work by Robin Lakoff (1975) suggested that in Western society women's language actually differs from men's language; she identified several linguistic features that she claimed were used more often by women than by men. For example, Lakoff maintained that women use more hedges, use very polite forms, use tag questions, speak in italics, use empty adjectives, use hypercorrect grammar and pronunciation, use *wh*– imperatives, speak less frequently, apologize more, overuse qualifiers, use modal constructions, use more intensifiers, and generally avoid coarse language. Lakoff believed that the reason women use these features is that women are uncertain, lack of confidence, and even lack a sense of humor. Other early research on interruptions and gender suggested that males interrupt more than females. In terms of feedback, early research suggested that women provide more encouraging feedback when having a conversation and are more cooperative in such conversations than men, who tend to be more competitive. Finally, in terms of the concept of gossip, early research pointed to different functions of gossiping for both genders; for women it is to affirm solidarity (i.e., for social purposes), whereas for men gossip was seen just as a discussion without personal feelings (i.e., for referential purposes). All of this research, of course, is upholds stereotypes, does not account for individuals, and does not account for transgender identities. In addition, although Lakoff is credited with the idea of women being marginalized in society because of the type of language they use (e.g., hedging), this was not based on any methodologically sound research; it was based mostly on her own observations. Janet Holmes became known for more robust research on language and gender issues within sociolinguistics and applied linguistics.

Holmes (2008) is perhaps most known for her work on language and gender in Western society, where she maintains that social roles of men and women overlap more, so she suggests that the speech forms also overlap. As a result women and men do not use different forms; they just "use different quantities and frequencies of the same forms" (p. 160). Holmes also notes that in non-Western societies this may not be the case and that in fact men and women may use different language. However, as mentioned above, the focus of much of this chapter is on language and gender in Western societies.

Holmes (2008) points out that across many social groups women tend to use more standard forms compared to men, and men tend to use more vernacular forms. This, she suggests, can be because women are more status conscious than men, and how they speak thus "signals their social class background or social status in the community" (p. 164). Also, Holmes notes that another explanation for why women use more standard forms of language is that society expects women to use language in a "better" way, showing "better" behavior than men. This can be observed in young children as well; boys' misbehavior is tolerated, whereas girls are more quickly corrected. As Holmes points out "women are designated the role of modeling correct behavior in the community" (p. 165).

In terms of gender identity, we now know that gender is socially constructed rather than based on any biological presuppositions, and as a result we now consider that different speech communities will have different ways of creating gender identity. Holmes (2008) makes a distinction between sex and gender; she maintains that sex is biological, whereas gender is "more appropriate for distinguishing people on the basis of their socio-cultural behavior, including speech" (p. 157).

Within TESOL, an interesting issue related to identity and language and gender was raised by research conducted by Gordon (2004) on the status of immigrant women and their access to English language learning in the United States. He examined how women and men from Laos redefined and restructured their identities in the United States and the interrelationship between their language learning and changing identities. Gordon discovered that Lao women experienced increased opportunities for enhancing their gender identities as they became more independent, while Lao men experienced a loss of authority. English language learning gave these women access to information about U.S. cultural attitudes, laws, and public benefits available to them so that they did not have to rely on their husbands. In the United States, Lao women were able to take responsibility for negotiating with social institutions by using more complex English than their husbands in the workplace because most of the workers in the company were also immigrants. As a result of this research, the TESOL profession recognizes that access for immigrant students, especially women, can be restricted by many factors, such as family duties of housework, child care, time constrains, and safety demands. As such, TESOL programs may need to consider how to redesign their curricula to consider immigrant women's needs and concerns with family by perhaps providing on-site childcare facilities in the school while they take classes or other such measures to ensure that all citizens are fully socialized into their second language.

Sunderland (2000), partly in reaction to the early research on gender, wanted to consider gender in language education in new, nondeterministic ways. Specifically, she focused on gender in classroom interactions and the amount and nature of attention from the teacher to both boys and girls because much of the early research showed male dominance in classroom interaction. In addition, Sunderland also looked at student-to-teacher interaction. Much research has found that male students tend to talk to teachers more than females do. However, such results can be criticized as the studies that produced them used different measures to examine gender differences in students' interactions with teachers. Nevertheless, recent research on gender and language education in non-Western societies has suggested that male dominance is still present in language classrooms. Hu (2012), for example, conducted a study in a senior high school classroom of 47 students in China, where he investigated whether teachers treated boys differently than girls and whether boys and girls behaved differently in the classroom. The findings show that the boys received more positive feedback than the girls. In an interview before the classroom observation started, the teacher explained to Hu that the girls were more active in the classroom and were more likely to contribute than boys. Thus, since the teacher had lower expectations of the boys, she tended to give them more positive feedback if their answers exceeded her expectations. In contrast, the girls received more negative feedback than the boys since the teacher's expectations were higher for the girls than for the boys. So we can see that teachers have an important role to play in English language classrooms in terms of gender and language.

The Role of TESOL Teachers

There are several actions TESOL teachers can consider in relation to language and gender both inside and outside the classroom. Teachers can try to avoid gender bias in their actions in several ways, such as designing and including activities that are gender neutral and age appropriate as well as reflecting on their practices and classroom behaviors toward students and whether they tend to favor one gender over another.

We cannot ignore gender because it impacts our students' social lives as well, so we need to be reflective about our understandings and prejudices so that we can take appropriate actions when necessary. Teachers can point out any gender bias they note in their textbooks, and this can generate healthy discussions about gender bias in society so that the class remains relevant to students' lives and does not ignore their realities outside the classroom. Thus teachers can organize their language lessons in such a manner that, at the very least, encourages students to understand that gender bias exists.

Awareness raising about how to avoid stereotyping in English language lessons can be as simple as pointing out to students that, unlike other Indo-European languages, as Folse and Vitanova (2006) demonstrate, in the English language grammatical gender is marked in a few nouns, pronouns, and possessive adjectives, and the traditional grammar lesson involves learning the forms (e.g., *actor/actress*, *he/she*, *his/her*). Folse and Vitanova note, however, that nouns that may have male/female counterparts tend to use only one form. Thus, they point out that *actor* is preferred regardless of the gender of the person. *Flight attendant* (instead of *steward/stewardess*), *chair* or *chairperson* (instead of *chairman/chairwoman*), and *host* (instead of *host/hostess*) are the standard, nonsexist terms. Having to learn only one form for a person's occupation or role—as in doctor, teacher, lawyer, or nurse—is easier for second language learners, according to Folse and Vitanova.

In addition, gender and language can be specifically included in language lessons, particularly in English grammar. Folse and Vitanova (2006) note that students need to be taught that in English, sexist language is something that should be avoided since there are social and cultural influences that are demonstrated through the grammar of the language. As they point out, "Modern scholars believe that there is not a direct relationship between language use and gender. Instead, researchers have argued that each community constructs gender in a different way" (p. 54). This means that sociolinguistics is concerned with not only gender identity issues, but also specific linguistic features with the language and specifically, according to Folse and Vitanova, sexist language. Folse and Vitanova present the following two paragraphs in which they contrast changes made in the text of the second one from the first in order to make it easier to understand and to lessen any possible confusion related to grammar and gender issues. The first paragraph reads:

> When a student finds a word, he or she has to think about the word's possible meaning from the context if he or she does not know the meaning of the word. If there is time, the student can consult his or her dictionary, but what if he or she finds this word during a timed reading activity? (p. 55)

The second paragraph, with changes underlined, reads:

> When students find a word, <u>they</u> have to think about the word's possible meaning from the context if <u>they</u> do not know the

meaning of the word. If there is time, the student<u>s</u> can consult <u>their</u> dictionary, but what if <u>they</u> find this word during a timed reading activity? (p. 55)

The second paragraph is shorter (49 words in length vs. 58 in the first one), and the fewer words leads to fewer chances of making mistakes. The changes in the second paragraph help avoid student confusion related to *he/she* and *his/her*. The most common verb error by ESL students is forgetting the –s for the third person singular. Using *they* solves this problem. In addition, the changes address the sexism in the language of the first paragraph.

REFLECTIVE QUESTIONS

- What do you think of the way Folse and Vitanova (2006) attempted to manipulate grammar in order to remove sexist language?

- Is it a good solution for teaching gender? Can something else be done?

Conclusion

This chapter outlined and discussed issues related to language and gender in English language teaching. Some early "research" suggested that women may have been disenfranchised in society because of their language use, and later work by Holmes pointed out that women and men tend to use different types of language. In addition, the chapter indicated that language teachers should try to point out gender bias in English language textbooks and teaching materials and monitor lessons for any classroom interactions that may be male dominated. It is important also that issues related to gender and language not only be brought up in classrooms but also be covered in TESOL teacher education programs. Of course, there are many more issues that could have been covered, but limitations of space would not permit this.

CHAPTER 5

Identity in Language Learning and Teaching

The previous chapter discussed the issue of gender identity in terms of expressions of and motivations for learning English, especially as immigrants in the United States. For many second language (L2) learners of English, that move from their home country to the destination where English is used as a first language can be full of instability and difficulties as they begin to develop a new identity in a new social context. As Wenger (1998) has noted, identity develops in day-to-day experiences that occur through participation in communities of practice. This identity development, according to Pavlenko and Blackledge (2004), can be *imposed* and thus not negotiable, *assumed* and accepted but still not negotiated, or *negotiable* and thus changed by the L2 learner. This chapter outlines and discusses the issue of L2 learner identity as well as TESOL teacher identity within the realm of sociolinguistics.

Identity in Language Learning and Teaching

When students whose first language is not English first encounter the learning of English as an additional language, they cannot really avoid the issue of learner identity (be it imposed, assumed, and/or negotiated) because they must participate in a community different than what they are used to. An interesting study by Morita (2004) provides a good example of how L2 students from Japan negotiated their membership and identities in new academic communities in a Canadian university. A common identity illustrated by the Japanese students was being less competent than other local students because they said that they could not fully understand reading materials, lectures, and classroom participation rituals. In addition, these students often constructed this identity based on the ways other peers perceived them. However, some of the L2 students began to negotiate their identities, and one student in particular employed several strategies such as preparing items to talk about before class and asking instructors questions after class.

Although Morita indicates that L2 identities can be negotiated rather than remain static, there are examples in the literature where this was not the case. Liu's (2002) study, for example, showed how Chinese students constructed their L2 identities through silence in the language classroom. These students were concerned with losing face if they gave incorrect answers to teachers' questions, so they listened attentively instead of orally participating, and this was part of their identity as L2 learners. That said, the students still had high academic achievement scores, whether or not they spoke during the L2 class. The research indicates that TESOL teachers should be aware of the cultural differences students bring to their classes and that L2 students will experience different challenges and struggles when attempting to develop new identities as L2 learners while gaining membership in a different community of English speakers. In some cases the L2 students may need guidance from their TESOL teacher, especially if they construct identities based on how they think others perceive them rather than their true reality of what identity they want to negotiate.

Connected to the identity of L2 learners is how TESOL teachers see themselves and the various roles that are imposed, assumed, and/or negotiated while they teach in different settings. In addition, teacher identity includes how teachers are seen as TESOL teachers by others and as such influences decisions made by the teachers themselves in the L2 classroom. Throughout their careers teachers construct and reconstruct (usually tacitly) a conceptual sense of who they are (their self-image), and this is manifested through what they do (their professional role identity). Farrell (2011) has suggested that reflecting on teacher role identity gives language educators a useful lens with which to view the *who* of the teacher and how teachers construct and reconstruct their views of their roles as language teachers in relation to their peers and their context. Farrell's case study identified 16 main role identities divided into three major role identity clusters: teacher as manager, teacher as professional, and teacher as "acculturator." This last cluster may be unique to ESL teachers, and it supports Duff and Uchida's (1997) findings about language teachers as cultural workers: "Whether they are aware of it or not, language teachers are very much involved in the transmission of culture, and each selection of videos, newspaper clippings, seating plans, activities, and so on has social, cultural, and educational significance" (p. 476). Indeed, this role identity cluster puts ESL teachers in closer proximity to their students than would normally be the case for teachers of other subjects such as math or science. So TESOL teachers, who are often the first contacts for newcomers in ESL situations and cultural informants in EFL situations, play a key role in not only helping to construct their L2 learners' identities but also determining how they want to construct their own identities as TESOL teachers.

The Role of TESOL Teachers

TESOL teachers can play a crucial role in not only identifying but also helping to transform L2 learners' identity and perhaps encouraging their involvement in classroom participation. At the very least, TESOL teachers can reflect on their own L2 learning experiences as well as their intercultural experiences and identity formation and then revisit their classroom teaching practices with these reflections in mind. In this way, TESOL teachers can be sensitive to their L2 students' identity formation and development so that they can develop identity options for their students not previously envisioned. The fact that some L2 students' construct their identities through silence may be a result of culture or gender differences, but it may also be because of the format of the course and/or lesson, the TESOL teacher's choice of lesson activities, pressures from other classmates, or any number of other complex issues at play. The more a TESOL teacher reflects on such possibilities, the more he or she can become more aware of L2 students' identity formation and factors affecting classroom participation. By becoming more aware of the communication and interactional patterns in their classrooms, TESOL teachers can be advocates for inclusion rather than exclusion and thus embrace diversity rather than fear it. In this manner, both L2 learners and TESOL teachers can continue to develop and shape their identities appropriate to their circumstances.

REFLECTIVE QUESTIONS

- What is your understanding of Pavlenko and Blackledge's (2004) three identities: imposed, assumed, and negotiated?

- Are you an L2 learner of English? If so, did you experience any of these identities, and if so, how did you feel?

- How can L2 learners of English negotiate their identity through silence?

- Do you think that TESOL teachers' role includes that of teacher as cultural worker?

- What is your understanding of the identity role of teacher as acculturator?

Conclusion

This chapter focused on the identity development of L2 learners and TESOL teachers. As L2 learners enter a new community of practice when they learn English as a second or foreign language, they inevitably take on an identity different in some manner than when in their L1 community. This identity is more pronounced when L2 learners have moved to a country where the L2 is used as a first language. In this case, L2 learners can have an identity imposed, assumed, or negotiated. TESOL teachers as well can have identities imposed, assumed, or negotiated, so for both L2 learners and TESOL teachers it is a good idea to first articulate their identities and then reflect on whether this is in fact their true identity as learner and teachers or whether they need to (re)negotiate it to their desired identity.

CHAPTER 6

Language Planning

Language planning is a large area of sociolinguistics and as such impossible to cover in great detail in this short book, let alone this chapter. Nevertheless, it is a very important part of the macro part of the field because it can have such a huge impact on countries, governments, education, institutions, and ordinary people. Language planning originally developed as a concept to solve language problems as people and governments tried to find alternative means to solve these problems. This chapter discusses language planning and the role of English language teaching professionals.

Language Planning

In a seminal article on language planning, Ricento and Hornberger (1996) outline different frameworks and approaches for language planning as well as the role of English language teaching professionals in shaping language policy. In particular, they address policy planning and cultivation. Policy planning focuses on macro society and nation issues associated with standards (perceived or otherwise), while cultivation focuses on language literacy issues at the micro level. They also note three types of planning:

status, acquisition, and corpus. Status planning focuses on language use, acquisition planning addresses language users, and corpus planning pertains to the language itself.

That covers the *planning* within language planning. Now we look at the *language* within language planning. In this context, language can be viewed as a problem for minority groups who are not integrated into society. It can be viewed as a right whereby local language(s) is seen as important for their speakers' identity. Language can also be viewed as a resource whereby local languages are considered resources not only for the speakers, but also for the entire society.

Ricento and Hornberger (1996) note the importance of the different layers of planning and policy, such as legislation and political processes, states and supranational agencies, institutions, and finally the classroom practitioner. At the national level, policy objectives are developed and political decisions are most influential for language planning issues, as these become modified and have to be implemented at lower levels by agencies that begin to shape and affect (positively or negatively) language planning to serve their particular interests depending on their resources. The next layer of language planning and policy are the instructions that dictate how planning and policy will be implemented and evaluated within these institutions. Finally, we get to the lower level of the process, the classroom practitioners who, according to Ricento and Hornberger, should be the heart of language policy because they are on the front lines of implementing any educational decisions made at all the other layers by policy-makers.

Although classroom practitioners are said to be at the center of planning and policy implementation, they are not always consulted, and this can have detrimental results as discovered by Farrell and Kun (2008). Farrell and Kun studied how Singapore English teachers' beliefs and attitudes toward the use of Singlish in language classrooms affect their feedback on students' oral performance. The focus of the study was to find out whether there was correlation between language teachers' beliefs and their actual teaching practices regarding the official "Speaking Good English" language policy launched in Singapore that opposed the use of Singlish because it is nonstandard English. Farrell and Kun's findings reveal that teachers have different beliefs about the appropriateness of using Singlish in classrooms, which results in different teaching practices when it comes to providing feedback on students' oral performance. Therefore, the study indicates that there is a gap between the ideal language policy and teachers' actual beliefs,

Sociolinguistics and Language Teaching

and teachers' reactions to the language policy are complex. This shows that TESOL teachers have an important role to play when implementing language planning and policy that impacts their practice.

REFLECTIVE QUESTIONS

- Examine the different layers of language planning and comment on why the classroom teacher is the last (or lowest).

- Why do you think Farrell and Kun's (2008) study of Singaporean teachers showed a gap between the official language policy and teachers' actual beliefs?

The Role of TESOL Teachers

When it comes to language planning and policy that impacts TESOL teachers' practice, it is important to reflect on several considerations. First, in the classroom, teachers' day-to-day decisions are shaped by society and in turn shape social order, and as such TESOL teachers should reflect on what their main influence will be when considering needs: their students' needs or society needs? At the heart of this issue is the fact that TESOL teachers are not only individuals teaching ESL or EFL but also role models, advisors, and cultural informants for their L2 students (see also Chapter 5) and as such can impact language policy on a daily basis in many different ways. In fact, TESOL teachers (as noted by Farrell & Kun, 2008) can modify such policies through actions in their classrooms and institutions, especially if they think these modifications will lead to improvements. Conversely, English language teaching professionals can oppose language policy and refuse to implement it if they think it is detrimental to their students' and communities' future, not to mention their nation's future. In addition, TESOL teachers can become proactive in co-constructing and recreating language policy that better meets the needs of their students, community, and society, and this can begin in their classrooms by reflecting on their actions so that their students will be successful.

Conclusion

This chapter briefly discussed the important issue of language planning and the different layers involved in such planning. It pointed out that language teachers unfortunately are rarely included in language planning or policy but are usually charged with implementing it in their lessons. Unless the top layers involved with language planning and policy directly consult the teachers who have to carry it out, the planning and policy will be carried out in a haphazard manner depending on the teachers' beliefs as well as the students' understanding of such policy.

CHAPTER 7

Reflecting on Sociolinguistics and Language Teaching

There are many ways to gauge how students interpret sociolinguistics and language teaching, such as regular quizzes, essay writing, examinations, and the like. One nontraditional way is to give students a reflective position paper about the course. I have done this in the past with a course called Sociolinguistics Applied to Language Teaching, which emphasized similar topics in the field of sociolinguistics: language choice in multilingual communities, language maintenance and shift, linguistic varieties, language planning, language and gender, and so on. I asked each student to write a reflective position paper that answered the question: What is the importance and impact of sociolinguistics for my future as a language teacher? I analyzed all 13 assignments, and (with the students' permission) I now report on some of the students' reflections, in most instances in their own words (Farrell, 2015).

One of the major outcomes of the reflective assignment is that all 13 students remarked that they had been deeply impacted in some way by taking this course. In addition, all 13 also noted that they now considered this subject matter very important for all language teachers, but they did not know this before taking the course. In fact, many students had never heard of the word *sociolinguistics* before. As one student wrote:

Before this class, I had never heard of, been exposed to or discussed sociolinguistics. In fact, I now realize that good teachers should not only know the learners' language level based on whatever tests, but also each individual learner's sociolinguistic repertoire. The language we teach is not just mechanical and cannot be extracted from society that surrounds it. This coexistence influences the language learning as well as teaching.

One student who had taken an introductory undergraduate socio-linguistics course noted the impact of her prior learning experiences on her reflections as a result of taking my course and how these reflections will shape her future teaching philosophy:

> This sociolinguistics course gave me the opportunity to reflect on my past experiences as a language learner. The moment I knew that I wanted to be a language teacher, it became my mission to ensure I provide a safe and comfortable learning environment for my students.

However, this student said that she was not sure how to implement this knowledge, except for telling her students it was normal to make mistakes while learning a language. Then she said that as a result of taking this course she realized that language learners' role in "the target language community would affect language learners' identity. This is an area that is not typically given much attention, but it certainly plays a role in the shaping of language learners' identity." This student also said, "Sociolinguistics allowed me to build on my teaching philosophy." She went on to note how taking such a course in sociolinguistics and applying it to language teaching

> served as a reminder to look at my future learners as diverse individuals who come into the classroom with their own unique history and experiences. It has also allowed me to reflect on my teaching philosophy and build on it to better reflect this new perspective of my future learners.

Other students in the course also commented on the impact of the course through the reflective assignment, highlighting such issues as code-switching, power relations, English varieties, and language maintenance.

Code-switching

A number of students, especially the international students, related to the topic of code-switching both from the students' perspective and the teachers' perspective. For example, an international student noted that when she arrived in Canada there were some English as a second language schools that had an established English-only policy in all classes and they effectively banned code-switching by the students. She said that she found this policy ineffective and isolating for her because she was not able to express her thoughts and as a result began "to feel incompetent in the L2 [second language]." The student explained that this school that prevented students from using their first language (L1) in classes also instituted particular punishments to enforce this rule:

> The student who is caught using his or her L1 is subject to certain punishment. Some of these punishments are a red card given by the teacher, suspension from the school for 1 to 2 weeks, and if the student does it more than once he or she will be expelled. The school system also bans the use of electronic dictionaries.

The student went on to note that she stayed silent during her lessons because she was afraid of using her L1:

> As a result, I remained silent most of the class only because I did not understand most of the terms and consequently, I became hesitant to participate with the wrong information or meaning of the terms. This incident affected my self-confidence because I was not sure about the right answer.

As a result of her readings in the sociolinguistics course, she realized that allowing only a monolingual ESL classroom can have severe effects on students' self-esteem because they may not be confident about speaking in English and therefore remain silent, effectively being excluded from the class. The student said that as a result of her experiences and reading in sociolinguistics, she will allow her students to code-switch in the classroom "regardless of the 'English Only' policy that may or may not be in place."

REFLECTIVE QUESTIONS

- Do you think it is good language teaching to ban students' L1 in the classroom?

- What do you think about the idea of giving a red card to a student who uses the L1 in the classroom?

- Do you think that not allowing students to use their L1 in the classroom will have a negative impact on their self-esteem?

- Will you code-switch as a teacher (if you speak your students' L1)?

- Will you allow your students to code-switch (even if you speak or do not speak their L1)?

Power Relations

The topic of power relations is somewhat broad and used here to encapsulate a few interrelated issues such as language and gender, language and identity, diversity, and ethnicity and language power and discrimination. One international student captured all of these issues in her reflection:

Sociolinguistics has helped me understand my role as a future teacher in scaffolding my students and providing them with cultural, social, and lingual responsive classrooms, which on the other hand highlights my responsibility towards understanding their different backgrounds, religions, social and political values that may affect their language learning experiences and levels.

Another student noted that taking the sociolinguistics course helped her bridge the gap between herself as a woman from the Middle East, whose experience is being influenced by gender, culture, ethnicity, religion, and nationality to different extents and at different times, and as a learner in a foreign country that finds herself the "other" to many people while negotiating her new social and cultural space.

Although she noted that she has experienced some difficult cultural adjustment moments in her new country (Canada), "sociolinguistics has increased my understanding and acceptance to my learning experience, lowering my anxiety and negative attitudes towards the various difficulties that I experience in a new different place, while trying to adapt and express myself."

Just as in this book, in the sociolinguistics course most of the topics and issues covered were intertwined with each other (although each one was treated separately each week), and this was certainly true of power relations and language. One student summarized how gender, language and identity, diversity, and ethnicity and language power and discrimination are all connected:

> Understanding power relations between the different genders and ethnicities, in addition to the power that English has over other languages, increased my sensitivity and responsibility towards thinking about various strategies to best involve all students in a comfortable environment while maintaining their individual space.

REFLECTIVE QUESTIONS

- What is your understanding of power relations in language learning and teaching?

- How can TESOL teachers provide classrooms that are responsive to students culturally, socially, and linguistically?

English Varieties

The topic of different varieties of English in the course inspired many interesting reflections from students. One student realized that before he came to Canada all of his "foreign" English language teachers were from the United States and were teaching American English, which was considered the "standard English" for him. He had assumed that if he studied this "standard" he would have no communication problems with English speakers, but this was not to be the case as he experienced when he first travelled away from his home country:

> When I went to a conference in Hong Kong, I found it was difficult for me to understand English speakers who were not from America and British. When I came to study in Canada, I found it was hard for me to understand some people who were not native here, such as a taxi driver who was an immigrant from India.

He noted that these experiences and the sociolinguistics course readings made him reconsider this issue. He wondered, for example, why his English language education teachers "never gave me a chance to expose to English varieties other than British English and American English" and, as a result of these reflection, whether he would "teach these varieties to my students." He continued:

> For example, if my students are planning to study in North America or they think they might contact foreigners from North America more in their work, I think it is necessary to introduce vernacular languages that are used relative frequently in North America. Although it might violate the curriculum objectives, I believe that learners need to be exposed to those frequently used varieties other than "standard English," which will provide them an opportunity to [become] familiar with the real-life communication.

REFLECTIVE QUESTIONS

- What is your understanding of "standard" English?
- What variety of English were you exposed to?
- What variety of English will you teach to your students?

Language Maintenance

A final important topic from the course that impacted some students' reflections was language maintenance. One student said that when she started reading on this topic in the course she began to connect her own experiences as a bilingual Canadian to the importance of maintaining a language in a community where not everyone speaks it. She reflected on how difficult it is for families who are bilingual to continue to use both languages when the school system discriminates against the use of any language other than English (or French in some parts of Canada):

> I had an immediate personal connection to it because as a bilingual speaker born in Canada, I feel I have had some similar experiences to the children of immigrants in Canada. As a child, my family spoke [the home language other than English] in our home, but were advised by school administration to use English instead for the sake of my future English capability. Luckily, this simply was not possible because of the limited English proficiency of my grandmother, who was my primary caregiver. In the end, I was proficient in both languages.

As a result of the course readings on language maintenance, language shift, and language death, she realized how influential the school system can be when discouraging multiculturalism and multilingualism in the home:

> Often school administration takes the approach that English-only both in school and home environments is the best option for children. However, this can be at the cost of the family's dignity and pride in their home language and culture. Not only that, but also a feeling of being silenced by not being able to express inner thoughts and feelings due to lack of L2 proficiency. If children are led to believe their L1 is inferior or useless, they may grow to resent their parents' culture.

This student said when she is a teacher in future she will support bilingualism because through "both the L2 through focused language lessons and the L1 by encouraging use in the home, children can grow to be functionally bilingual, which appears to have many benefits for them, both cognitive and practical."

REFLECTIVE QUESTIONS

- What is your stance on bilingualism?
- What is the TESOL teacher's role with bilingual students?

Although the student reflections included in this chapter give only limited and particular examples of how specific students were impacted by topics such as prior learning experiences, code-switching, power relations, English varieties, and language maintenance, in fact all the students thinking about their future careers as language teachers seemed to have been changed in various ways. As one student noted:

> Sociolinguistics is a crucial source of knowledge for all language teachers because it helps teachers become more equipped and knowledgeable of how best to present the language for their students while maintaining an understanding of the various elements that may govern learners' attitudes, beliefs and knowledge.

Indeed, some of these reflections were serious for individual students and had profound implications for them personally and professionally. As another student realized:

> Before studying sociolinguistics I used to blame myself for taking various identities or even switching codes. My main concern was to preserve my first language and identity. Yet understanding that code-switching and multiple social identities are normal and constituent parts of the process of learning a second language has encouraged me to appreciate the change and accept it as a bridge towards social and lingual integration since identities are usually complex, multiple, and subject to change. I have now only come to realize this and it really makes me feel relieved.

REFLECTIVE QUESTION

- What are the importance and impact of (name of course) for your future as a language teacher?

References

Bayyurt, Y (2013). Current perspectives on sociolinguistics and English language education. *Journal of Language Teaching and Learning, 1*, 69–78.

De Angelis, G. (2011). Teachers' beliefs about the role of prior language knowledge in learning and how these influence teaching practices. *International Journal of Multilingualism, 8,* 3, 216–234.

Dewaele, J., & Wei, L. (2014). Attitudes towards code-switching among adult mono- and multilingual language users. *Journal of Multilingual and Multicultural Development, 35,* 3, 235–251.

Duff, P. A., & Uchida, Y. (1997). The negotiation of teachers' sociocultural identities and practices in postsecondary EFL classrooms. *TESOL Quarterly, 31,* 451–486.

Farrell, T. S. C. (2015). Encouraging critical reflection in a teacher education course: A Canadian case study. In T. S. C. Farrell (Ed.), *International perspectives on English language teacher education: Innovations from the field* (pp. 36–50). Basingstoke, England: Palgrave MacMillan.

Farrell, T. S. C. (2011). Exploring the professional role identities of experienced ESL teachers through reflective practice. *System, 66,* 1–9.

Farrell, T. S. C., & Kun, S. T. K. (2008). Language policy, language teachers' beliefs, and classroom practices. *Applied Linguistics, 29,* 381–403.

Farrell, T. S. C., & Martin, S. (2009). To teach Standard English or world Englishes? A balanced approach to instruction. *English Teaching Forum, 47*(2), 1–7.

Folse, K., & Vitanova, G. (2006). Sociolinguistic factors in TESOL: The least teachers and teacher educators should know. *TESL Reporter, 39*(1), 48–58.

Gordon, D. (2004). "I'm tired. You clean and cook": Shifting gender identities and second language socialization. *TESOL Quarterly, 38*, 437–357.

Haukås, A. (2016). Teachers' beliefs about multilingualism and a multilingual pedagogical approach. *International Journal of Multilingualism, 13*(1), 1–18.

Holmes, J. (2008). *An introduction to sociolinguistics* (3rd ed.). Harlow, England: Pearson Education.

House, J. (2003). English as a lingua franca: A threat to multilingualism? *Journal of Sociolinguistics, 7*, 556–576.

Hu, W. (2012). Gendered EFL classroom interaction: A case study in a senior middle school in China. *Theory and Practice in Language Studies, 2*, 1818–1827.

Kachru, B. B., & Nelson, C. L. (1996). World Englishes. In S. L. McKay & N. Hornberger (Eds.), Sociolinguistics and language teaching (pp. 71–102). Cambridge, England: Cambridge University Press.

Lakoff, R. (1975). *Language and women's place.* New York, NY: Harper & Row.

Lee, J. H. (2012). Implications for language diversity in instruction in the context of target language classrooms: Development of a preliminary model of the effectiveness of teacher code-switching. *English Teaching: Practice and Critique, 11*(4), 137–160.

Lee, J. S., & Oxelson, E. (2006). "It's not my job": K–12 teacher attitudes toward students' heritage language maintenance. *Bilingual Research Journal, 30*, 453–477.

Liu, D., Ahn, G., Baek, K., & Han, N. (2004). South Korean high school English teachers' code switching: Questions and challenges in the drive for maximal use of English in teaching. *TESOL Quarterly, 38*, 605–638.

Liu, J. (2002). Negotiating silence in American classrooms: Three Chinese cases. *Language and Intercultural Communication, 2*(1), 37–54.

Macaro, E. (2001). Analyzing student teachers' codeswitching in foreign language classrooms: Theories and decision making. *Modern Language Journal, 85*, 531–548.

Morita, N. (2004). Negotiating participation and identity in second language academic communities. *TESOL Quarterly, 38*, 573–603.

Pavlenko, A., & Blackledge, A. (Eds.). (2004). *Negotiation of identities in multilingual contexts.* Clevedon, England: Multilingual Matters.

Ricento, T. K., & Hornberger, N. H. (1996). Unpeeling the onion: Language planning and policy and the ELT professional. *TESOL Quarterly, 30*, 401–427.

Shuy, R. W. (1969). The relevance of sociolinguistics for language teaching. *TESOL Quarterly, 3*, 13–22.

Sunderland, J. (2000). New understandings of gender and language classroom research: Texts, teacher talk and student talk. *Language Teaching Research, 4*, 149–173.

Wenger, E. 1998. *Communities of practice; learning, meaning and identity.* Cambridge, England: Cambridge University Press.

Young, T., & Walsh, S. (2010). Which English? Whose English? An investigation of "nonnative" teachers' beliefs about target varieties. *Language, Culture and Curriculum, 23*, 123–137.